MY GOD MADE ME

ABENA AFFUL

AuthorHouse™
1663 Liberty Drive
Bloomington, IN 47403
www.authorhouse.com
Phone: 1 (800) 839-8640

Published by AuthorHouse 01/11/2019

ISBN: 978-1-5462-3713-6 (sc)
ISBN: 978-1-5462-3714-3 (e)

Library of Congress Control Number: 2018904278

Print information available on the last page.

authorHOUSE®

My name is Brittany. God made me. He gave me a head with beautiful hair.

He put a brain in my head so I can think.

He gave me two eyes so I can see. I see beautiful things around me. I see the blue sky. I see the clouds moving slowly in the sky.

Sometimes the clouds are gray and sometimes they are white.

I see the flowers in the garden.

They are blue, red, green, and white. Some are tall and some are short. Each flower is so beautiful!

With my two eyes I see them all.

I see the parrots
and the crows.

I see the roosters and the hens.
The chicks run after the hens
flapping their yellow wings.

I see the trees. The coconut trees
are lined up on the beach.

The orange tree is different from the banana tree. They have different leaves and fruits.

A mango has a different shape than the grapefruit.

God gave me two ears. I listen and hear with my ears. I listen to Mommy as she reads to me every day.

I hear bees buzzing around the flowers.

I hear the dog barking in the street. hear cars moving along the road

When it rains, I hear the thunde rolling. It makes a lot of noise

I can't see the wind but I can hea it blowing. It blows so hard that th trees move back and forth

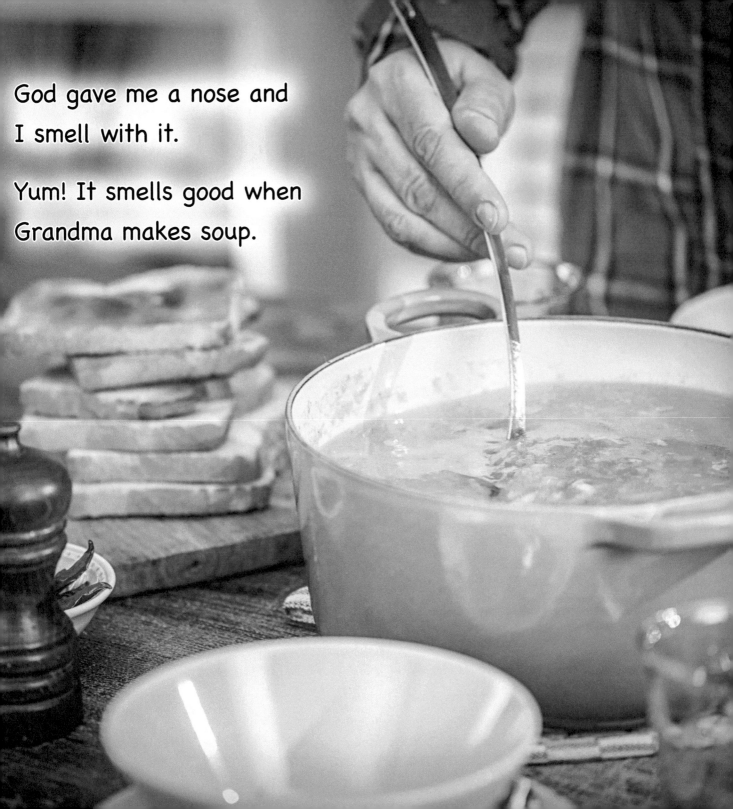

God gave me a nose and
I smell with it.

Yum! It smells good when
Grandma makes soup.

I smell the flowers and Mommy's perfume when she is all dressed up.

God gave me a mouth. I have a tongue and teeth in my mouth. I speak and I say good things with my mouth. I say "hello" to my friends and I tell the truth to my teacher.

I taste with my tongue and I know when food is sweet and sour.

The coconut fruit is so sweet. I love it.

I love fruits. They are good for me.
They make me healthy.

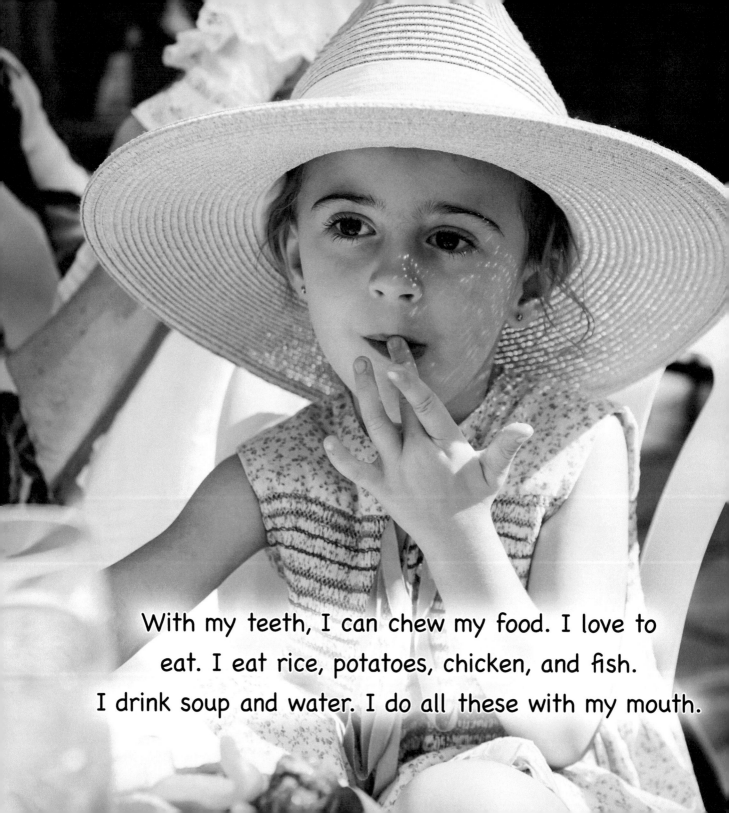

With my teeth, I can chew my food. I love to eat. I eat rice, potatoes, chicken, and fish. I drink soup and water. I do all these with my mouth.

God gave me two hands.
I have five fingers on
each hand. I hold my
books in my hands.

I brush my teeth and wash my face with my hands. I am happy when I raise my hands and praise the Lord!

God gave me legs so I can
run and walk. I walk as fast
as I can. I kick and jump and
dance. I dance like a queen
and I dance like a star.

I play soccer and many other games with my legs.
I have ten toes on my feet.

I am very beautiful!
God made me so!

Printed in the United States
By Bookmasters